From the Nuthouse and an Outdoor Existence

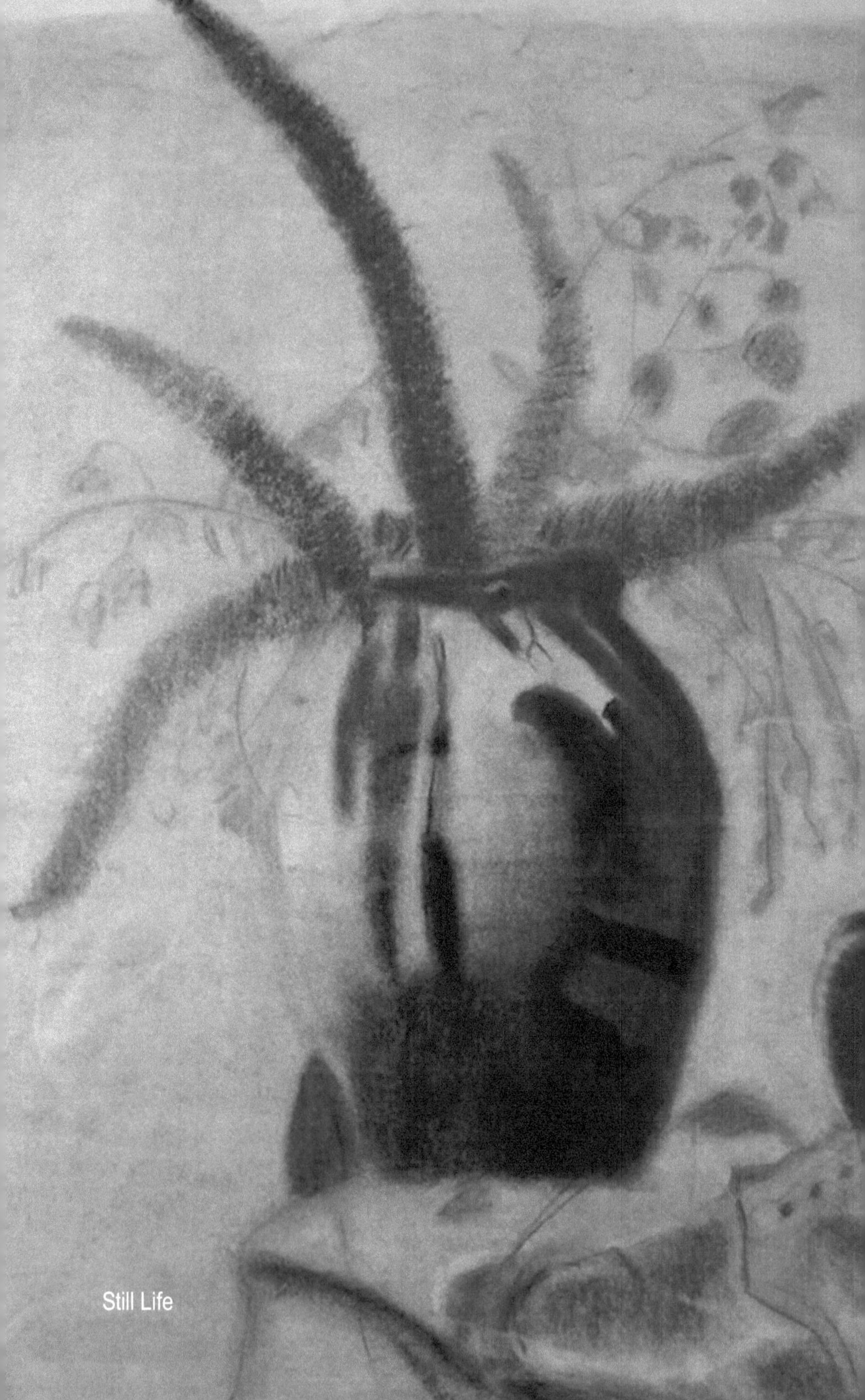

Still Life

From the Nuthouse and an Outdoor Existence

Poetry and pictorial art
by S.A. Reagan

ISBN-13: 978-0-578-42344-9

TABLE OF CONTENTS

PART 1: POEMS FROM INSIDE THE NUTHOUSE

PART 2: POEMS FROM AN OUTDOOR EXISTENCE

FORWARD

In the coming home from travel one experiences culture shock, not in answering the call to go forth. Arriving home from Europe/Asia Minor in 1974-77, brought me incredible growth, but also, pain for those around me. Struggling to claim my worldly ways ,in the face of authoritarian forces as the Vietnam War was coming to a close, was not anathema to that home for myself, others, and not soldiers whom I'd be-friended abroad. Orthomolecular health was becoming, fast, a chosen non-favorite of the American medical industries, making our lives more complicated. Photography can soothe and transform images that haunt our world. Poetry has, perhaps, even greater power to arrange for us what is necessary in the way of thought and action. With subsequent incarcerations and outdoor wandering these arts facilitated my...

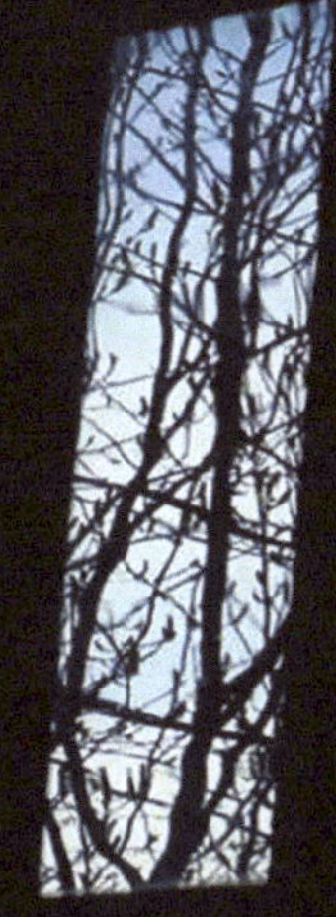

...becoming a survivor.

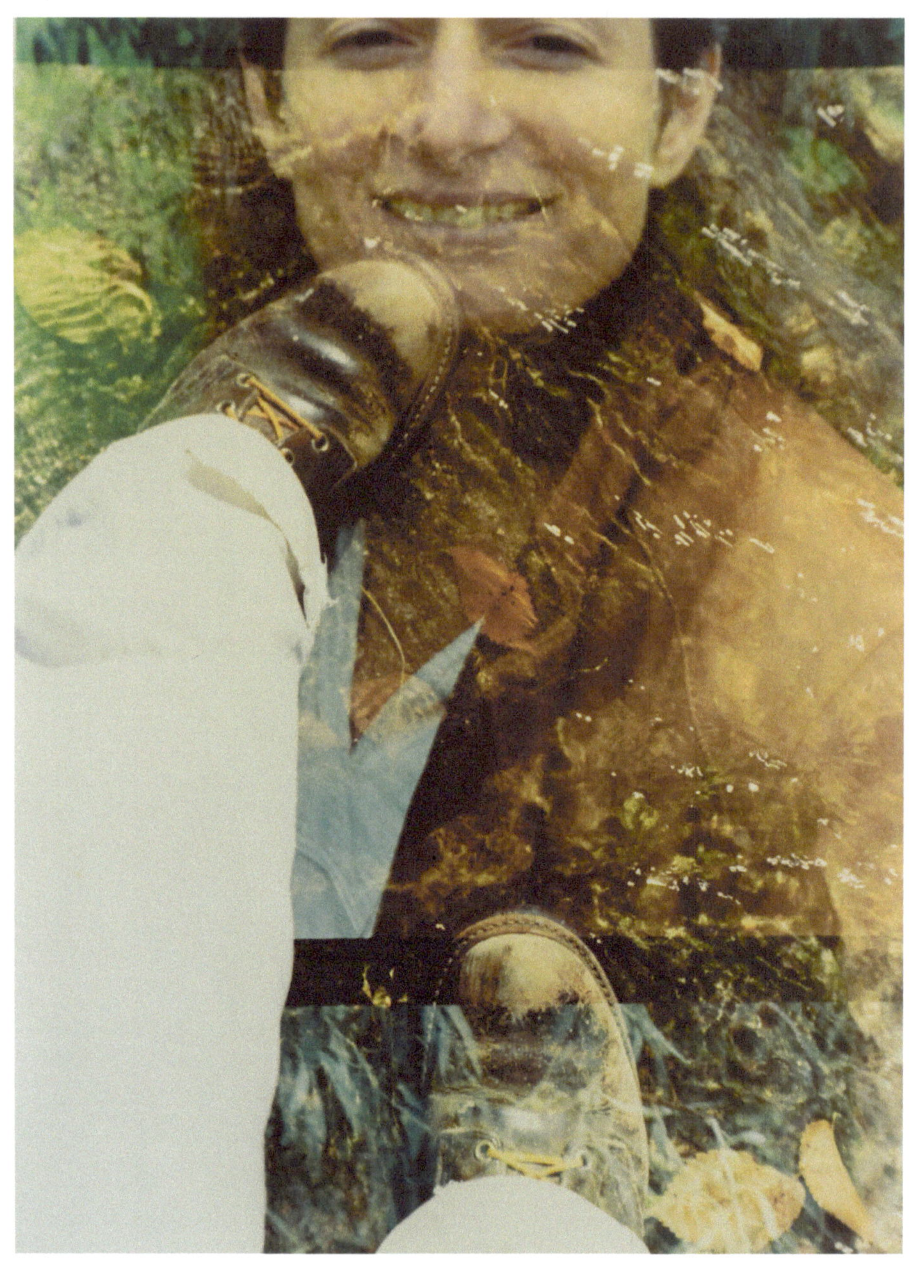

Reflections

Introduction

S.A. Reagan is an artist of words, songs, paintings, and photography. Her book, *From the Nuthouse and An Outdoor Existence,* is a compilation of her brilliance. She opens her heart to you and one finds a beam of creativity so unique that it defies a simple description.

I Found A Suicide Note is a poem-song that catches you off guard. "I found a suicide note; it was written by myself" is the first line of this lyrical poem. Who admits to contemplating suicide first of all? Then goes on to say she found the note; then confesses she was the author? A unique perspective.

Ms. Reagan's photographs, illustrations, and paintings express how we live alive in a world of color. Her paintings pop out with original shapes that spray rainbows everywhere. Her images go around the canvas like children at play; the energy jumps off the page. In her charcoals and oil stick paintings, the images are beautiful and the subjects fresh. There is an illustration of a vase with flowers; charcoal, simply titled, *Still Life,* where the light shines off the subject into one's eyes. There are abstract paintings that one absolutely loves with their unique shapes twirling all about.

S.A. Reagan survived a mental institution. She survived living outdoors. Now, she reflects on those experiences through her art. She has come to tell and show the reader the truth of what it was like for her during those hard times. Amazingly, she is full of hope, not only for herself, but for all of us, who have been incarcerated or left outdoors, and for those of us who have not been. S.A. Reagan's poetry, songs, illustrations, and photography are gifts to us all.

with love,
Ekau

Acknowledgements

I would like to give heart-felt thanks to many people; Katherine Ekau Hall, a partner for so much in this life, including the many details of happiness and here, the printing of her painting, *Ocean Luau.* I am grateful to the subjects of my portrait photography living amongst our other framed art, inspiring so much in our home of many years. My family, has been so remarkable in steadfastness and loving care. My sister, Betsy, an Acupuncturist in Oakland, left too early, but not before her blessed influence on our life. Another sister, Claudia, shared much of her publishing and design skills and generousity of heart. Molly Grevel, Scott, and Robin Reagan have been very supportive in this endeavor making it possible to create my poetry.

Thank you to professors and other mentors for influence and guidance particularly since the unknowns of childhood began to take shape in adult study.

Bay Area Alternative Press has been a wealth of volunteers, and ink jet printers that this project of a book of poetry has blossomed. Special thanks to Brigett (for top notch multimedia input), Talia, Joe, Nelda, Kefle, Anne, Nate, and other volunteers, and operation management.

PART I:

Poems from Inside the Nuthouse

1983

Dedicated to Delsturz

The Third Window-Laundry Room (iv)

Dancing in the hall doorway;
doing a number on the staff.
She smokes in the laundry;
as clear as the sky ain't blue
hallway.

Reflection of a sunset in that glass
across the way.
Those closeby birdies in
juniper berries;
green and blue.

Tumbleweeds...
No breeze,
no rain.

Cigarette half done,
I run a fake on her;
she drops it,
then mad wants another.

Me,
I hate cigarettes and coffee;
coffee makes my face boil.

≈

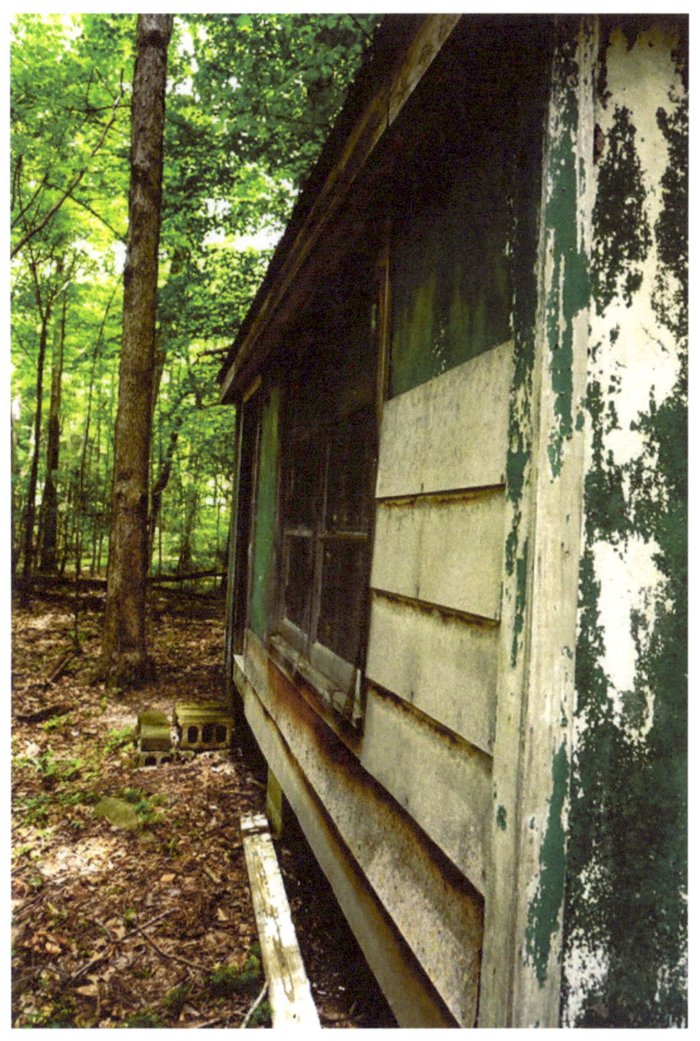

Penn's Woods Cabin

Wandering-Silent Saturday (viii)

Wandering the grounds–
My hour "out".
Saturday silent;
dead on the grass,
in the sun and out of…

I park it by the great
water tower.
Then, one other soul…
wandering.

I swing
alone,
as far as the eye can see…
state buildings,
thick, green, sprinklered grass
in this desert.

Jump off,
walk,
dead on the grounds by a picnic table.
Cool sweaty grass;
sticks to pop and pile,
leaves to crush so dry…
This is my job.

Returning to the ward;
the unit.
A whole group returns inside
another ward.

I stare...we stare
Waving,
he blows me a kiss;
two ships.

I press the buzzer
and wait for the
rattle of
keys.

≈

Two Crows (xii)

Two crows upon the ground
Outside.
Big black birds.
There are
other
bird feeders besides
the other windows,
which aren't open.
No more.
Washington and Roosevelt
and our ride towards Malibu from west L.A.
Outside that pool hall room window.
Outside that smokers' laundry.

≈

The Other Window-Day Room (iii)

Cheerios on the sill outside;
my bird feed.
And a bird I fed
from London, from Germany
and black.

Out the window on the lawn,
out the window on the walkway awning,
out the window, Cheerio.
Here birdie.

Tattling (xiv)

I'm tattling on you,
you would be smokers,
chasing after butts;
showing smoking
for what it is.

The elite smokers/pushers
don't like you
for that;
picking a butt
out of it's tray—it's final resting place.

Out of the waste and
betwixt those
God-given
lips...

"Got a light?"
"Got a match?"
Do you have fire?

≈

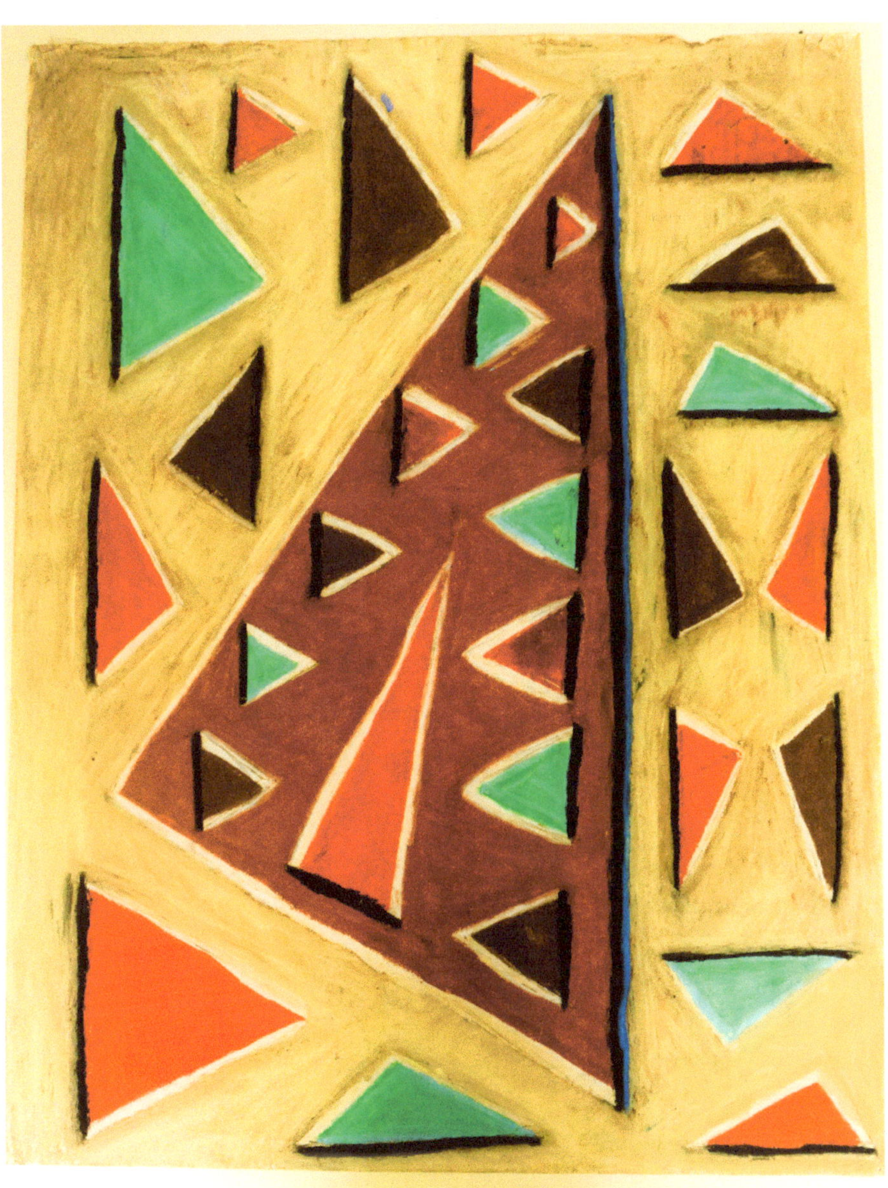

Triangular

Sitting By The Frog Pond (xxii)

Sitting by the frog pond
underneath a tree,
along came a cyclist
one cooling summer's eve.

Spinning on his wheels;
the day had lost it's hot,
"could we, could I'
____just around the lot?"

His and Cocoa's 'sport on wheels'
was sitting idle one day.
So, from that time and hence,
I've hopped it yelling, "yeah!"

Off in the sunset,
cycling out on two;
circling out these grounds,
until cooler winds did blew.

≈

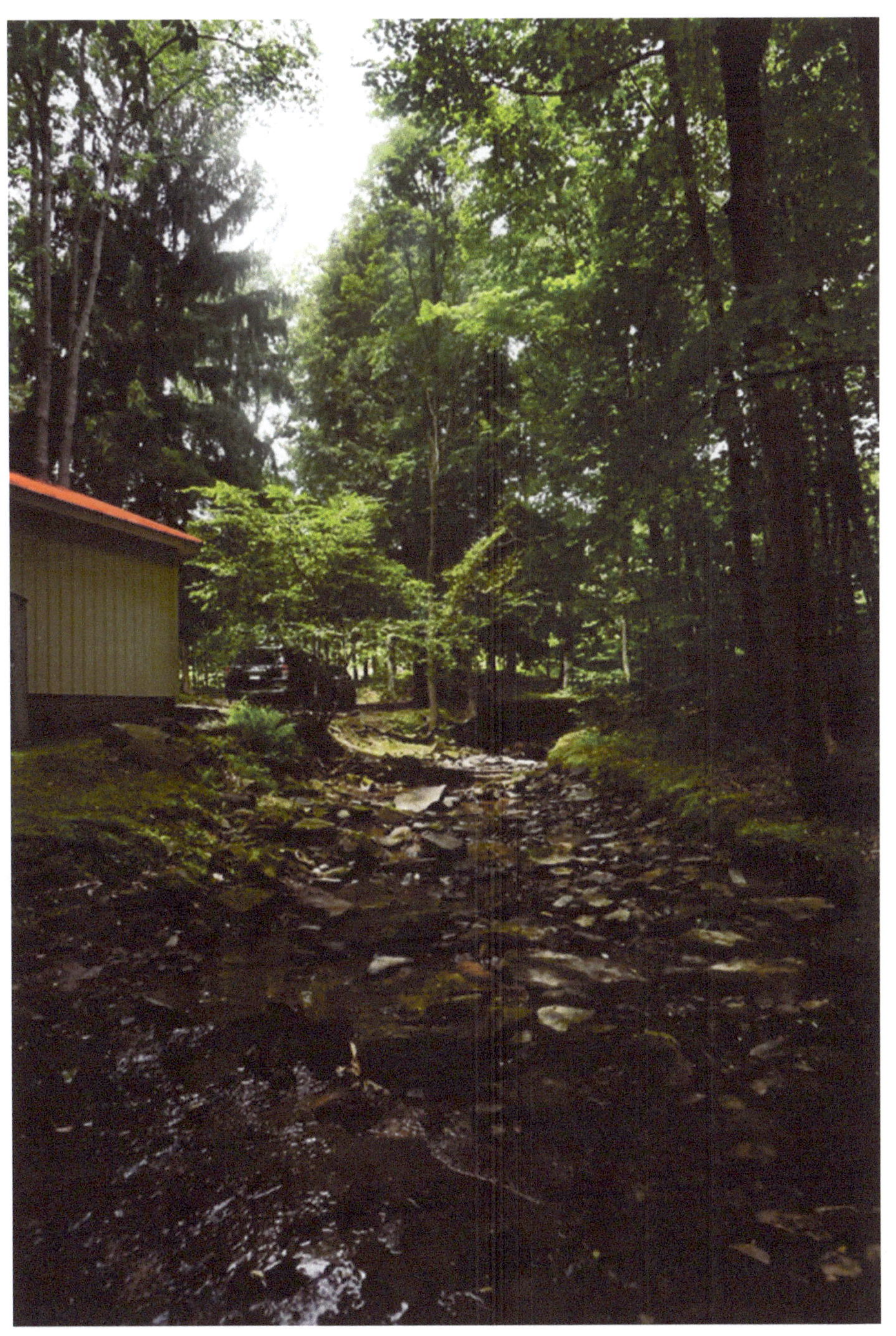

Laurel Run Creek

Wind Up-Chuck Went Out Today (xxiii)

Wind up,
gray skies,
autumn's lace, and
drops upon my face.

(Bruce left Friday),
Chuck went out today;
beyond these windows,
aspen leaf that he is;

beyond the walls,
beyond the bounds,
we three
walked yesterday.

Teethed up
Pueblo,
city strange to us;
as strange as
this place
and all it's haunts,
freaks,
heat and storm.

Home to
call it
Grand Junction.
Halfway house.

≈

Unkempt (xxix)

Unkempt.
We are;
motley.
Hair;
matted, ratty, greasy.
Socks … no shoes.
Clothing; unzipped,
over worn,
rumpled, spotted, torn.
Unshaved,
unbrushed, dirty
and John lost his staff keys.

So, it's
under "restriction";
TV off,
pool room shut....
We are;
unkempt, kept.
But that's unfair;
some of us
shower every day,
brush our teeth,
clip our nails______
change our clothes.

And don't steal keys …

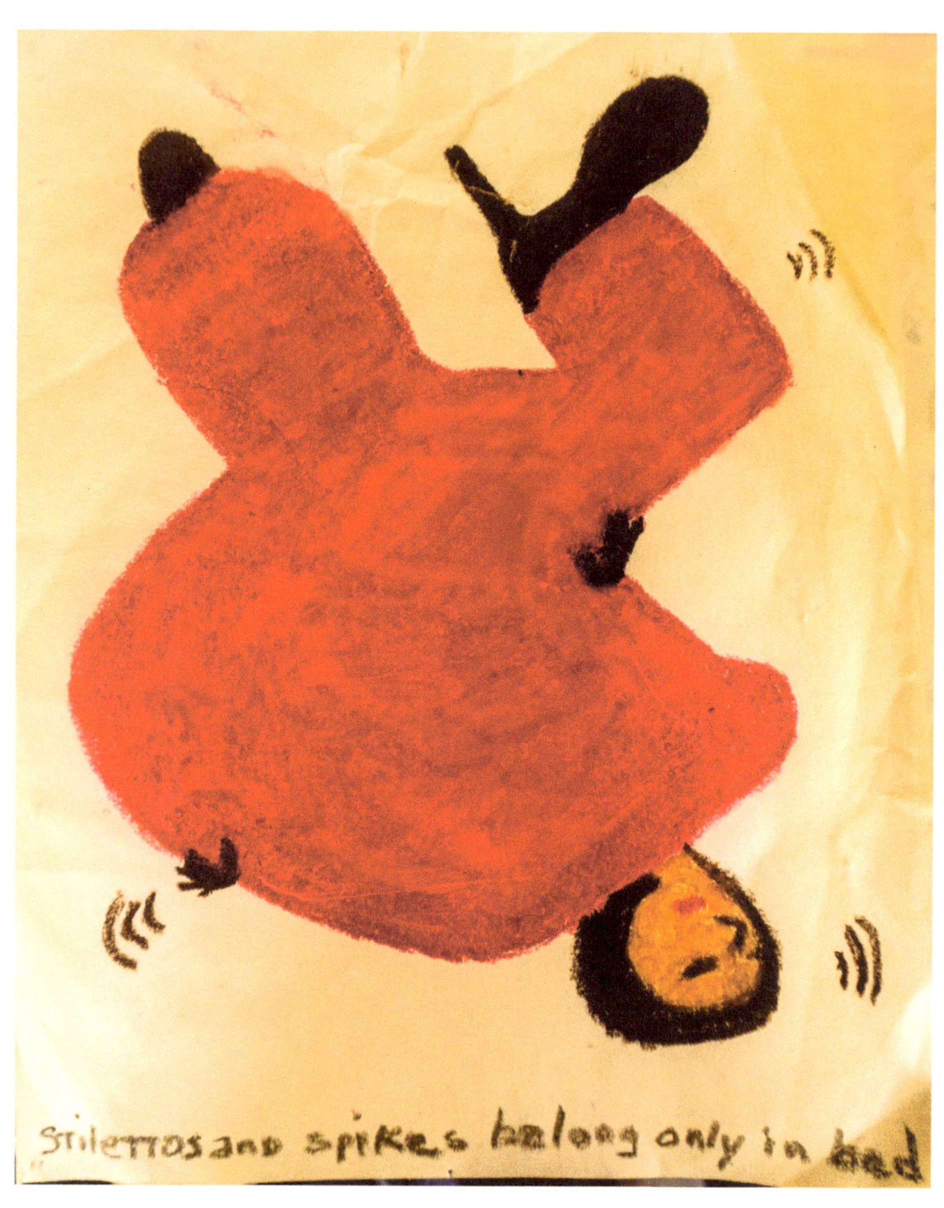

Stilettos and Spikes Belong Only in Bed

Pueblo's Gold

A golden light
fills up the
arbor way,
and I am
struck with fever;
veer off my path
to home and curfew.

I drink the light
as it
blindeth me;
gold as the corn
snitched from the
hospital garden
tasted in my
mouth,
tasted by the
ants.

Full blossom of sunlight
going down;
A jewel amidst the false greenery;
a jewel amidst the truth of the
mountains.

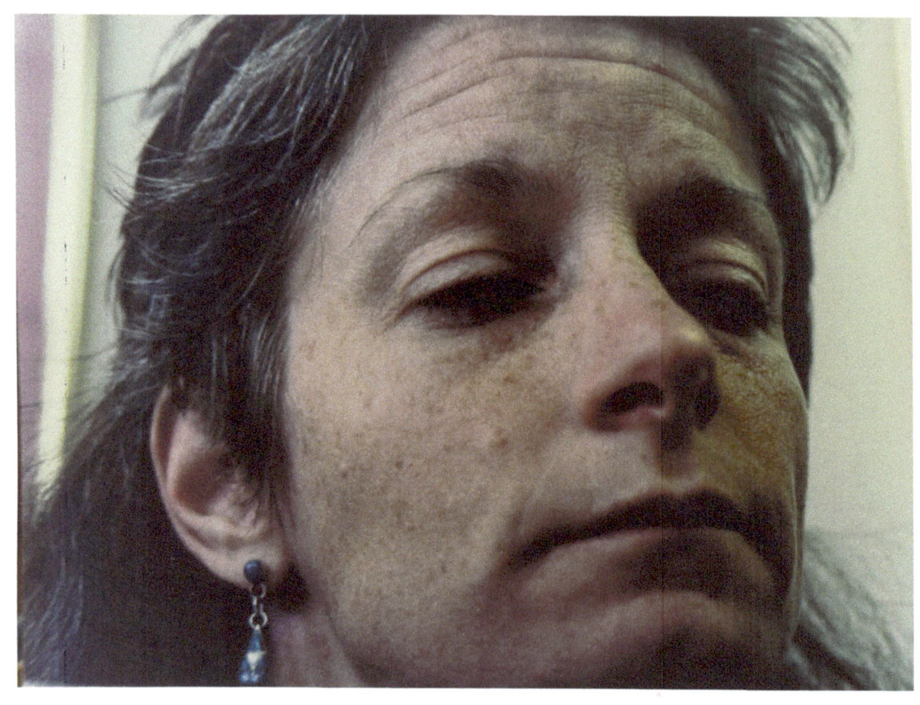

Stef 38 in '88

Part II

Poems from an Outdoor Existence 1990-91, 1995

Dedicated to my grandmothers:
Hazel Grubb Patton
Lela Wigglesworth Reagan

Fauna and Flora: Up Above the City and the Country

(Part I)

I lay down high above the peninsula'd sea
Karen's keys had found me; six months/
a year rusty.
Cuddling next to an upside-down running
belly-buttoned branch
I sought rejuvenation from that haunting me.

Nature called me out of the bag only once;
scribbling dreams of sight, I stayed tite to our Bush(sic)
Carving on the twig, I stayed another night.

But the jester suit went out of sight.

You are midnight daylight.

(Part II)

Winter Pansies shiver
at the base of a
tree.
Would that I have such
daylight in these
fox trot/rain gear
you see.

I’m learning to roll
at 40-41
a merciless tiny drum;
Peace watch
of an insidious nouveau war riche
just begun.

The streets have filled with
black and blood.
Signs show in the glass,
and ON THE ROAD[1],
and in the faces of people;
you and I.

Back against the trunk
Are you visionary?
Do you spend the day
out on a limb?

Maybe the pansies know
who’s next to go
in the rain forests
buggered by the paper cowboys.
Do we?

And do not the Hemperor, the DEA,
wear no clothes?

You are Midnight Daylight.

[1] Jack Kerouac, *On The Road: The Original Sroll*, ED: Penquin Classics Deluxe Aug 26, 2008

Goon-ey Tunes-for Ester-Know, for Diane America

Roll-y poll-y sniffing bee,
'n perhaps a porcupine, scuttering
about me.
Sleeping in the light;
to fend off the night.
I oiled up and down and in my hair a touch.
Soft, beside me,
a bee sniffed my shirt;
from late in the night
until the open pen-knife
curioused it worse.

Goon man beside me, my tooth
tube in a ditch.
I peruse the bay, everyday,
for the ship at sea;
wooden Picasso, square Lee.
Chant/smoking I might 'til gray
in my face.
Plainly,
I wonder at this door-mirror
staring on me.

The dick on the dark horse
came out so slowly.
He'd snorted at the garlic;
left it in the dirt…

Catherine told me in a great way
that love might hurt.
Eliza/Betsy Ross spread her blanket
there and then;
an oral chain ensued.
She readies death; makes no flag about it.
I love you 'cause you do-to-do.

Helio(copter) whistled down on me;
"don't forget to STOP THE WAR".
The quiet of the field
got raked up but not torn.
Here's the sound:
Helio to the left, out from
behind the hill,
back to the city-fill #550142 (Canon FT-QL).

And in my public joy, I thought
to send a toy to the wife of
~~Saddam Hussein~~ (Mr. Trump tower). A happy birthday
song in their toi-ty paper sing along!
Ding dong!

Marin or The Ability To Think On Your Feet

Sun on my back,
birds to the north,
my frog throat starting
to vibrate,
"NO MORE WAR".

Tubing on a river
where the sea
meets the shore.
There's fire now, where there was
smoke before.
I smoked a cig'rette.
I sucked it like a bitch.

So,
I need healing
and kneeling tall
outside this ditch
inside a brook.
I shake from Nico
the absense/presence of
ewe you
u-
turn.

≈

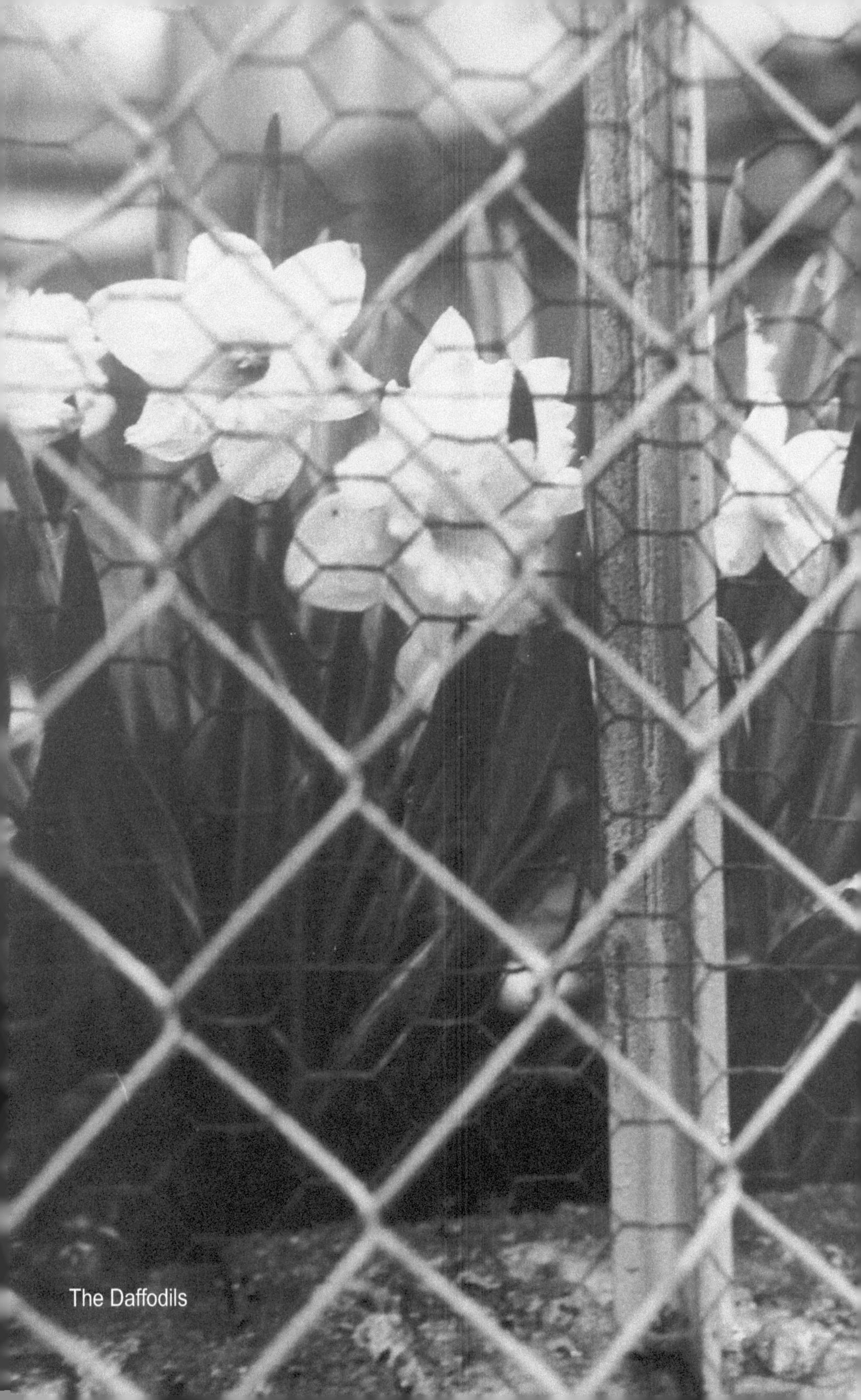

The Daffodils

Peace Watch (from Castro/Berkeley Year of the U.N.)

I sit here a-tappin' my cowlick
with a finger better left on it's own.
Others might find me busy
and choose to leave me alone.

Winter in Baghdad, Mo'gomery, San 'cisco's,
this peace we can barely grasp.
Poverty is war, only for the poor,
unless you've got some dash.

Babies, AIDS, and health care are
sometimes one and the same.
And about that dash and fortune;
I say it's a lie that "war ain't genicide",
Hey, come and sing our child's tune.

We need a U.N. peace just to survive.
So, I sit here a-tappin' my cowlick
with a finger, not after all, on it's own.
Others might find me busy
and join in together/alone.

Now, about that cowlick dream;
wherever we live and roam,
"let's get together" [2] the whole hand,
and play 'cause the U.N. can be our home.

2 Hayley Mills, *The Parent Trap* 1961

Homefree and War

Helicopter overhead, today.
Black clads are in the streets.
It's Saturday after, "STOP THE WAR",
There's not yet anything on my feet.

I found her keys beside me
while waking in the Bush (sic).
How would she lose them here?
Off the walk, beneath the tree?
Discord, war;
listen in these leaves.
"Do you want to stay the night with me?"

This Canon is quite broken.
sounds free my breath.
The rot of nationalistic plots and dots.
Constipated reason.
Dear baby dear doe season.

There are lovers who won't be
swayed away;
arm in arm,
the fay/the gay.

Bring on the new day
Welcome to the bay
Righteous sisters and brothers
Lay open a plan for home Spin.

17 Parts Tho Not Haiku

Chasing fresh winding
blacktop through
dark trees,
the fox darts;
splashing color,
deftly guiding,
fear, wonder, headlights.

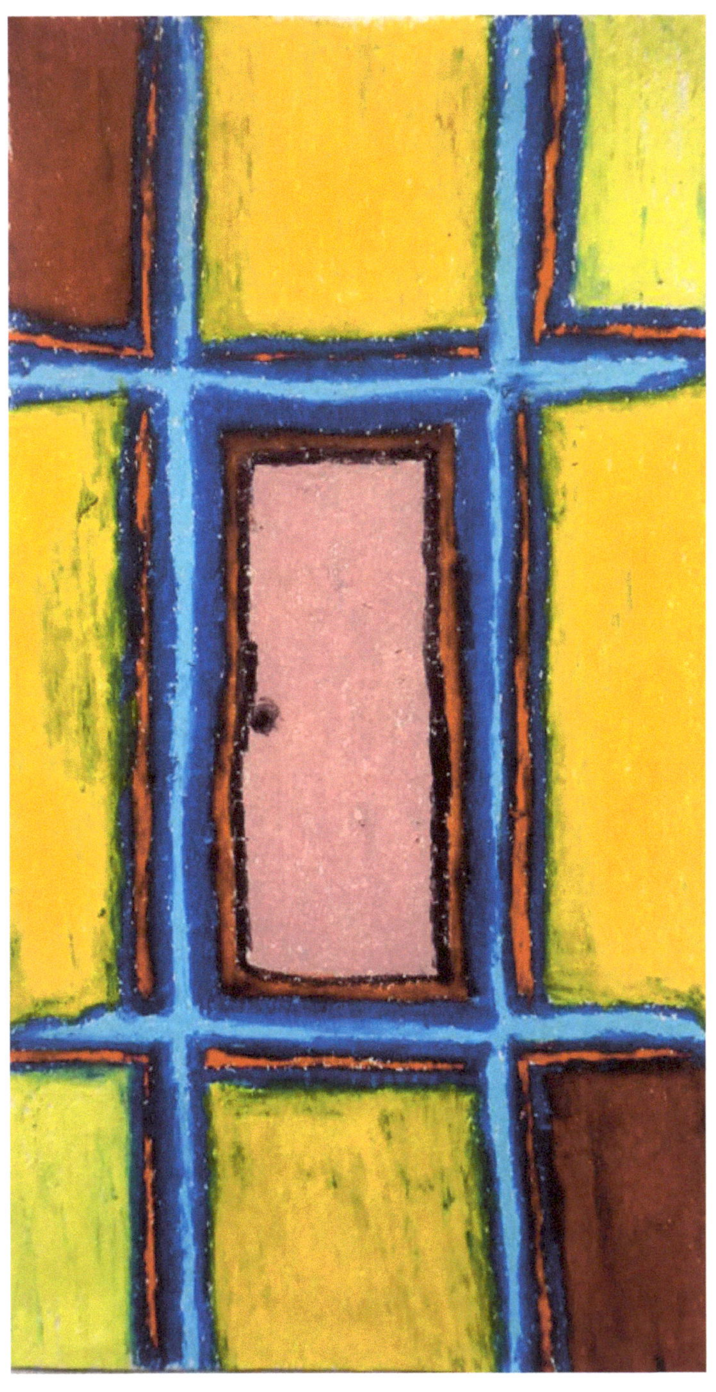

OpenADoorAndWalkInside

A Tear Runs Across

A tear runs across
the bridge of my
nose.
It tickles and so lightly
it hurt
(high voice) "ow ow ow".
-I spoke so politely-
The whole thing
made me
write right
light.

There's an art to
assembling
people.

≈

Lakewood

Give us this dot
our daily bread,
that manics
get our/his head
before breakfast
each time.
Forever;
Amen.

≈

Wash and Dry

Queer cunt
cousins spin.
Give me your seasonal winter
nachkiss (Deutsch) kisses
for I am a dish
wish which
spoons were
gay.
On what day? Any day.

≈

Less

There must be a Volkswagen that
lives around here.
The sound of it's wheels brings
me good cheer.
Just knock on a door and walk
inside.
Never give up the Dali play, but learn again
to ride.

≈

Elmo

Elmo got a haircut;

he's a dog,
you know.
He looks good and he doesn't;
he's a dog,
it'll grow...
Elmo got a trim.
He looks good but,
then again;
his ears
won't, anymore...
drag on the floor'.
He's no Vincent Van Gogh;
dog on a leash;
"Are you lookin' for sex?"
You run into police.
In the suitcase; his ear. T'fuzz, they let 'im
rob me of my China dress and Asian
souvenir.
A yogini ; left by my kind.
My treasures; unrestored,
and me; incarcerated.
Yogini? And
Houdini.

San Francisco's Gold

A golden light fills up
the waterway
and I am struck with fever;
veer onto my path for home and
curfew.

I drink the light
with the mind's of Yee.
Gold/black tunnel,
as the rings snatched
from my finger,
tasted in my sake'd mind.

Sunlight as the ring
square on his finger told;
amber pistols in this life not much
our own...

Medical miracle magic
returns myself to me, sublime.

Silver is my sense of you
when I'm/you're/we're
in realign.

I FOUND A SUICIDE NOTE

2 B sung

I found a suicide note
it was written by myself
I died and I didn't
I just had been zittin' on the shelf…

Too many times I've seen
that face around here
most of it being attached
Nowhere, no cheer…

Hey! Angels cry with us
in that paltry state.
Hey! Listen you, now,
to what they say:

There's always something
grand they's offering you
if you can accept a
compassionate change or two.

I found a suicide note
it was written by ourselves
We died and we didn't
we just had been zittin' on the shelf…

Too many times we've seen
those faces 'round here
most of 'em being attached to war;
nowhere, no cheer.

Hey! Angels cry with us
in that paltry state
Hey! Listen you, now,
to what they say:

There's always something grand
they's offering you,
if you can accept a
compassionate change or two?

I found a suicide note
it was written by our earth,
she died and she didn't
we just had been zittin' on her shelf.

Too many times they've seen those
looks around here
most of 'em being attached to war;
Nowhere, no cheer.

Hey! Angels cry with us
in that paltry state.
Hey! Listen you now,
to what they say:

There's always somethin' grand they's
offering you,
if you could accept the compassionate
change or two.

I found no suicide.

≈

OF THE BELOVED

2 B sung

Hey there's someone I'd like to keep,
sweet, sweet love makes me weep, leap,
sleep.
Touches my heart without any gloves.
Let's me in oh, please, please, please love.
Others may think life's a tilt-a-whirl...
but, I believe in a fiery curl...

Sweet, sweet, S A M ma'am, sweeter
than doves.
I'm learning, learning to love.
I have somewhere a heart of my own...
spend the center, just, searching the
home grown.
He takes me dancing; we step on the floor.
Down and up, there's music more and more.

World affairs are doing just great.
Hey baby, don't you hesitate.
what's a winter without any sleeze?
Freehand and heart; tease, tease.
I give him champagne when we get near.
Sake and milk make mama dear.

When I was 5, I loved the jungle gym.
Here comes my love, heap, heapin'.
Love is a giant, I am told;
there's so much glory to behold.

Take a step, you can walk for awhile,
with a smile, you can walk for many mile.
Hey there's someone I'd like to keep,
sweet, sweet love makes me leap, leap, leap.
Sweet this love; sweeter
than doves.

CARING COMES FIRST. YES, KNOW
IT DOES.

≈

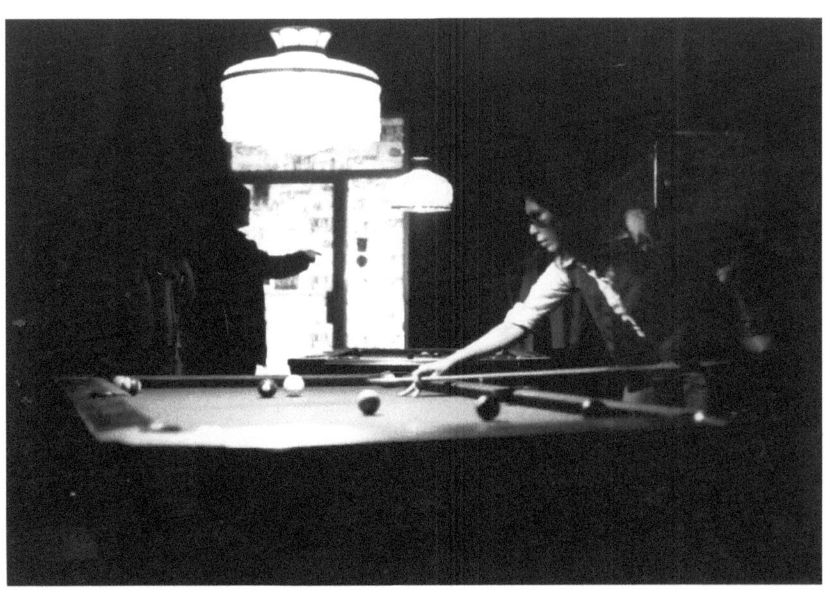

Sharon M. at The 19

SHE SELLS SEA SHELLS/COUNTING CARS FOR SHEEP (Golden Gate Bridge)

2 B sung

Helicopter overhead;
the dance is on the bridge.
Cars are stop, then go;
native on the ridge.

Sun going down;
daughters coming up.
Calling everybody to the bridge…

It's a rain dance;
a peace prance.
Calling everybody to the bridge…

Colorado's Schroeder found me dancing on the bridge.
Her warriors know that life can wane too thin.
But, she took my hand so we could grow old-young-old.
Calling everybody from/to the bridge.

(salute!)

≈

Katherine Ekau Hall

Ekau fierce and loving
calls me in from the "outside"
with her heritage begun as,
"Troubadours of the
South Seas", spreading warm moves
with voices sweet and so high in her
father, Spence's register.

They took their message as far into the
snow country
as any heart might go;
Chicago, Florida, and Minneapolis;
so much in our lives does co-inside.

From history to herstory alike;
we work our piece of rock and pie.
We learn and teach the lesson
"pawn to queen, each day".

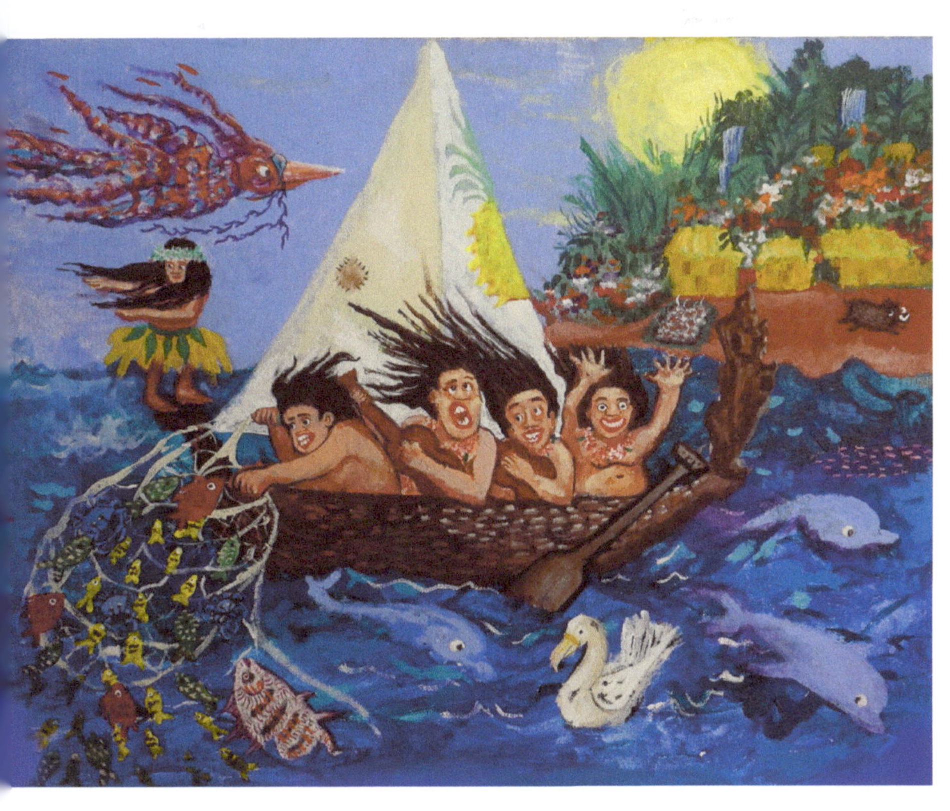

Ocean Luau, by Katherine Ekau Hall

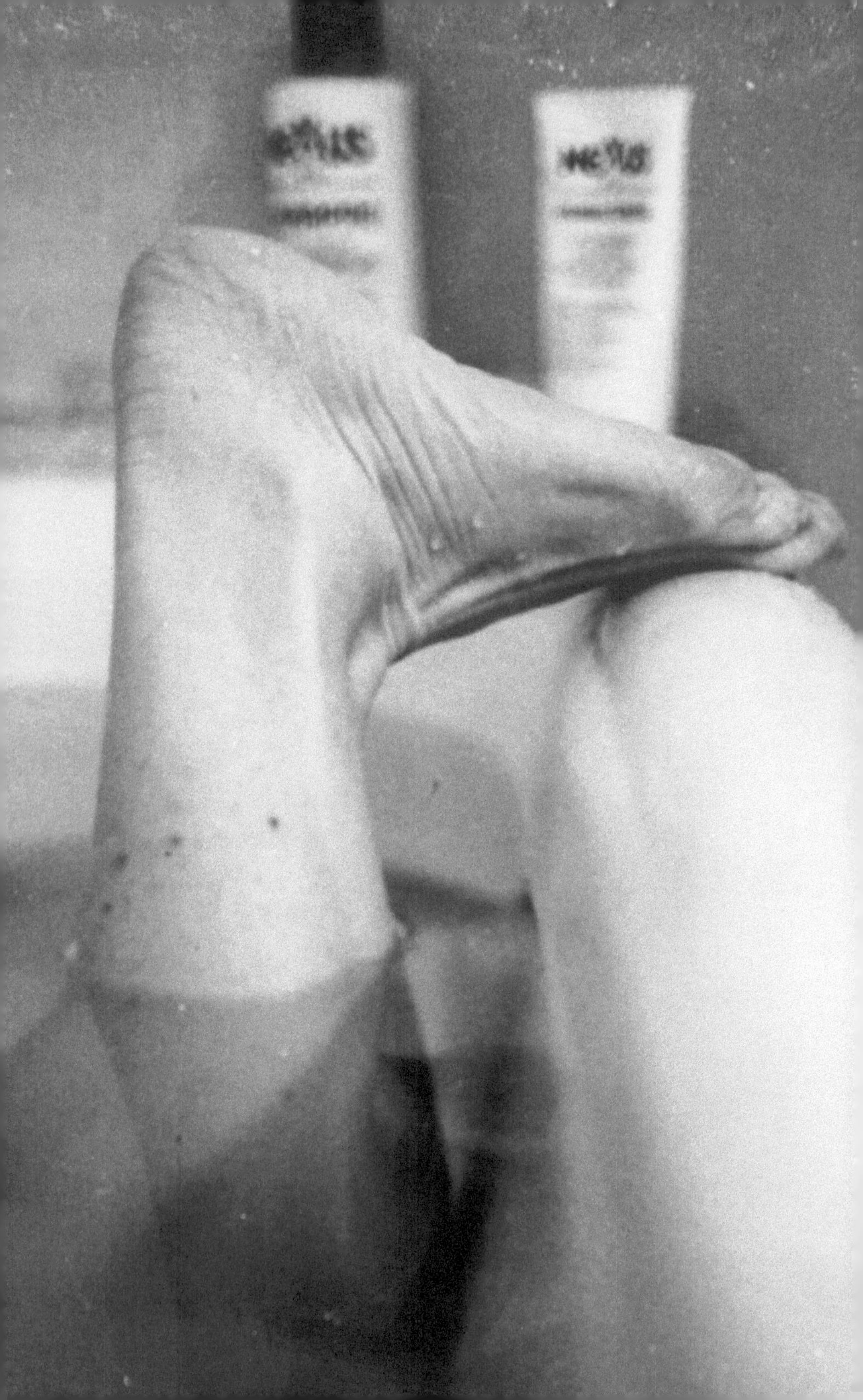

Pictorial Art

All art is by S.A Reagan, unless otherwise noted.

≈

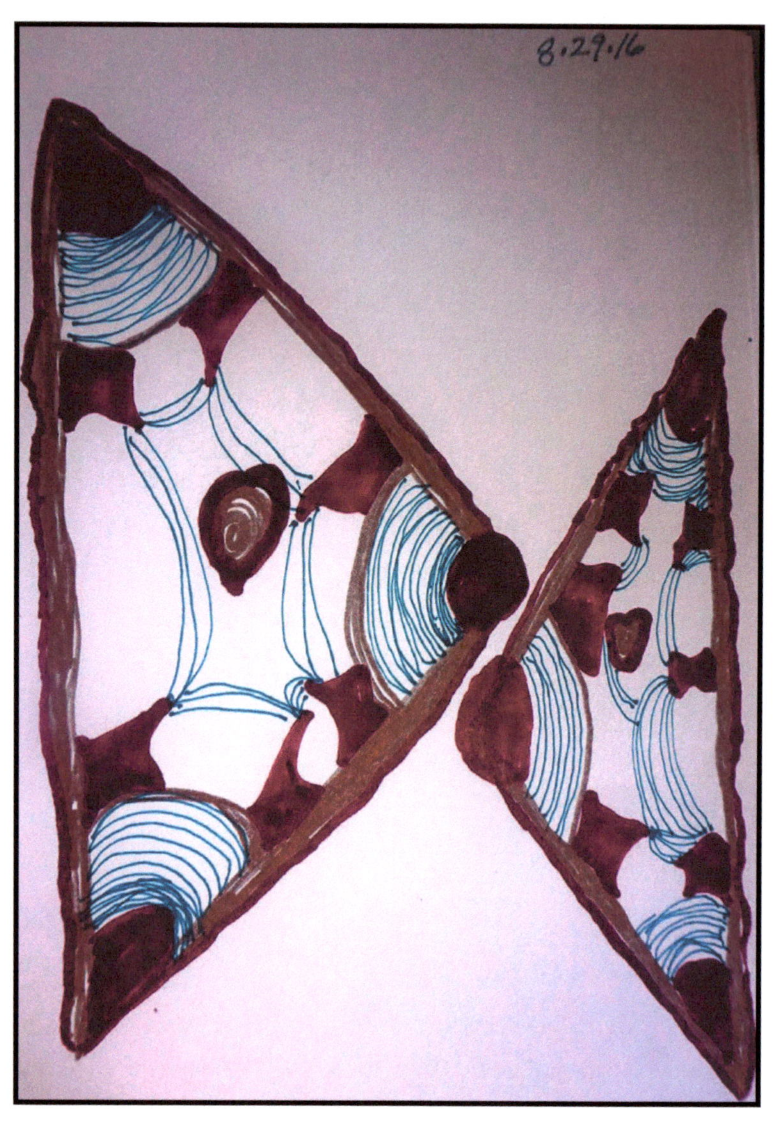

Introversion

About the Author

S.A. Reagan comes from a large family. In her youth during the 1970's she traveled to Europe and Asia Minor where her experiences en-kindled wonderous life change. Upon returning to America she was troubled by the authoritarian forces she found around her.

Becoming disabled in 1982 and finding interest in other than her own culture, she non-the-less gravitated to the streets. With persistence, overtime, she found her way to well-being despite some disappointments of health awkwardly thrust upon her. Stefanie trained and ran a marathon in Honolulu in 2006. She continued with education as was available in Colorado, and California; learning much else, culturally, in N.M., Baja California Sur, and Hawaii. In school she studied studio arts most recently, and graduated in the Spring of 2017 with three Associate degrees from Laney College. Presently, she is a member of the Digital Art Collective of Berkeley City College and often exhibits Photography in East Bay galleries and various venues. Her poetry has become more central in work on this endeavor and her life has taken on higher purpose in all endeavors.

Ms. Reagan and fellow artist, Katherine Ekau Hall, collaborate on many art projects and have had a business, Screamingheads, where they learned much about sharing their art and talents. . She lives in Oakland, California with Katherine and their cat, an American bobtail. They drove an Art Car, a 1970 VW, that is still held in high esteem around the Bay Area.

Labor Partially Donated

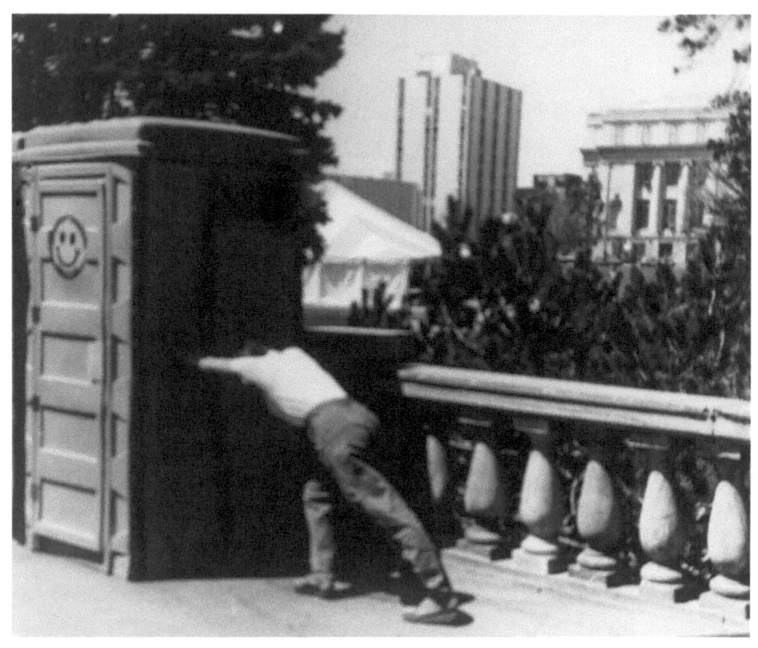

Stef and

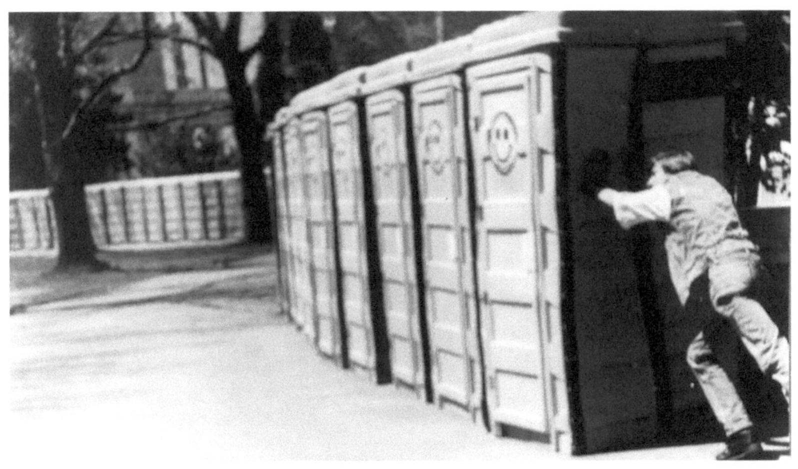

Erik Push

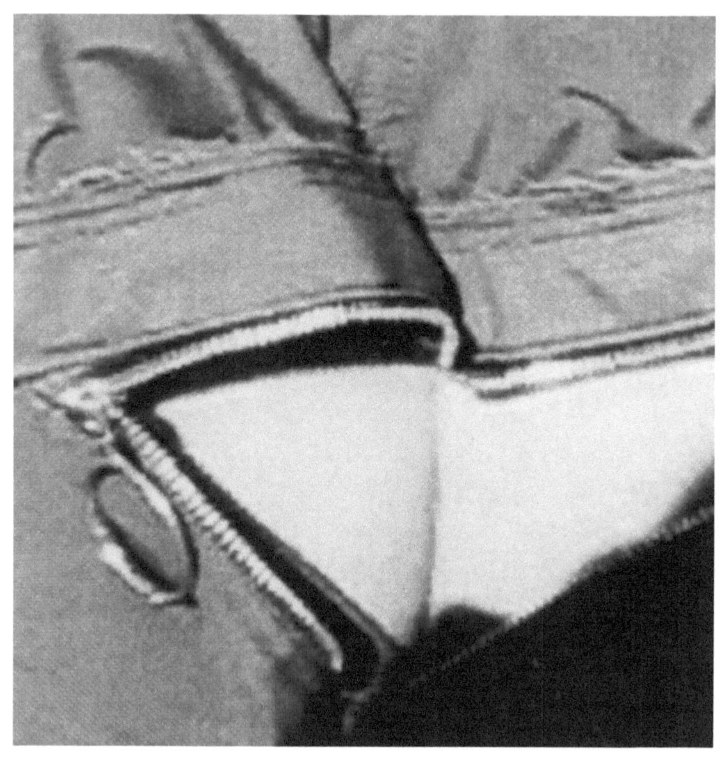

The End

www.ingramcontent.com/pod-product-compliance
Lightning Source LLC
LaVergne TN
LVHW052309100826
845147LV00006B/715

* 9 7 8 0 5 7 8 4 2 3 4 4 9 *